cheap & cheerful LOW-FAT SOUPS

Joan Yates Stewart

**FREEDOM FROM FAT FOREVER
BOOK I**

Copyright 1995 by Freedom From Fat Forever
All Rights Reserved

Edited by: **Martha Dinsdale-Thomson and Jackie Marrie**
Written and Published by: **Joan Yates Stewart**
Freedom From Fat Forever Ltd.

Canadian Cataloguing in Publication Data
Yates-Stewart, Joan, 1938 -
   Low-fat soups

(Freedom from fat forever; bk. 1)
ISBN 0-9680368-0-5

   1. Soups. 2. Low-fat diet–Recipes. I. Title. II. Series: Yates-Stewart, Joan, 1938 - Freedom from fat forever; bk. 1.
TX757.Y37 1996   641.8'13   C96-910064-7

Printed in Canada

ACKNOWLEDGEMENTS

I wish to express my heartfelt thanks to Jackie Marrie and Martha Dinsdale-Thomson for helping me publish this book; and my family, for believing in me and supporting me in my new venture.

INTRODUCTION

The mission of this cookbook is Healthy Eating and Creative Cooking with Low Fat. These soup recipes will show you how to cook with low fat and that you don't have to sacrifice taste for healthier eating.

It really is very easy - so easy that I wanted to share my recipes with you. You will never miss the fat once you learn to substitute with other ingredients. Reducing fat reduces a great deal of flavour. By replenishing recipes with herbs and spices we delete the fat and replace the flavour.

This cookbook focuses on soups. Everyone loves homemade soups - they are filling, nourishing, cheap, cheerful and easy to make. With few exceptions, they can be made ahead and frozen for the next week. Soups are great as a weekend lunch or an evening supper, served with your favourite bread (without butter, of course). Just dunk the bread in the soup!

I will share many low fat secrets with you along the way which can be adapted to any low fat cooking. For example, skim evaporated milk is my best friend for cream soups; it has a good thick consistency, yet doesn't have the high fat content of cream.

The spray oil I use is vegetable oil.

**Low fat cooking is a lifestyle choice that
is healthy and easy to accomplish.
Let's get hooked on low fat!**

ALL SOUP STOCKS USED IN THIS BOOK ARE MADE FROM POWDERED MIXES
BECAUSE THEY ARE LOWER IN FAT.

ABOUT THE AUTHOR

Joan Yates-Stewart graduated from the Culinary Arts Program at the internationally recognized Northern Alberta Institute of Technology, Edmonton, Alberta, in 1993. Under the tutelage of the superb chefs at the school, the two year program started her on her way towards developing her own specialty and skills in decreasing the fat content of traditional French cooking.

Joan demonstrates her talents in many different public engagements. She teaches a low fat cooking class at a local gourmet food store; teaches at various schools for the Board of Education's Continuing Education Program; speaks at many club and association events; does private catering and menu planning consulting for local restaurants. Additionally, Joan appears regularly on a television show which is broadcast provincially and throughout Canada. She is an associate member of the Canadian Federation of Chefs and Cooks.

Despite her busy career, Joan always has time for her three grown children and her first grandson who are all very excited about her move into print!

TABLE OF CONTENTS

BEAN SOUPS 7

COLD SOUPS 17

 CREAM SOUPS 29

MEAT SOUPS 39

 PURÉE SOUPS 57

SEAFOOD & FISH 71
SOUPS

 VEGETABLE SOUPS 85

INDEX 104

Chapter 1

BEAN SOUPS

AMAZING MEDLEY BEAN SOUP 8

BLACK BLACK BEAN SOUP 9

FENNEL AND WHITE BEAN SOUP 10

GREEN AND WHITE BEAN SOUP 12

LENTIL SOUP 13

LENTIL AND BROWN RICE SOUP 14

SEVEN BEAN SOUP 16

ALL SOUP STOCKS USED IN THIS BOOK ARE MADE FROM POWDERED MIXES BECAUSE THEY ARE LOWER IN FAT.

AMAZING MEDLEY BEAN SOUP

8 cups	water	2 L
1 cup	black eyed beans, dried	250 ml
1/2 cup	red lentils, dried	125 ml
1/2 cup	brown lentils, dried	125 ml
1/4 cup	split peas	50 ml
6 cups	prepared vegetable stock (powdered)	1.5 L
1/3 cup	onions, chopped	75 ml
1/3 cup	celery, chopped	75 ml
2 tsp	basil	10 ml
1 tsp	black pepper	5 ml
1/4 tsp	cumin	1 ml
1/4 tsp	garlic salt	1 ml
1/8 tsp	ginger, powdered	.5 ml
1	bay leaf	1
2/3 cup	white rice, uncooked	150 ml
1 cup	frozen corn	250 ml
2	green onion tops, chopped	2

Wash beans, lentils and peas and combine with 8 cups water in soup pot. Boil for 5 minutes. Drain. Add vegetables, stock and spices. Bring to a boil. Cover and simmer for 45 minutes. Add rice and continue simmering for another 45 minutes. Remove and discard bay leaf.

Season to taste with salt and pepper.

Garnish with chopped green onion tops.

SERVES: 6   FAT per serving: 0.5 g

BLACK BLACK BEAN SOUP

8 cups	water	2 L
2 cups	driedblack beans	500 ml
1	large onion, chopped	1
1/2 cup	celery, chopped	125 ml
1/2 cup	carrots, chopped	125 ml
2 cups	prepared vegetable stock (powdered)	500 ml
3	green chilies, diced	3
3 cups	brown rice, cooked	750 ml
1/4 tsp	ground black pepper	1 ml
2 tbsp	balsamic vinegar	25 ml
1	raw carrot, grated	1

Bring beans to a boil in 8 cups of water and simmer for 2 hours or until soft. Sauté onion, celery and carrots in balsamic vinegar until crisp and add to the beans.

Add vegetable stock, chilies and pepper to the bean mixture. Simmer for 15 minutes. Remove from heat and add cooked rice.

Garnish with grated raw carrots.

SERVES: 6   FAT per serving: 0.2 g

To make vegetable or bean soups thicker, purée one half of the mixture in the blender, then recombine.

FENNEL AND WHITE BEAN SOUP

1 tbsp	olive oil	15 ml
2	cloves garlic, minced	2
1	small onion, diced	1
2	celery stalks, diced	2
2	medium carrots, diced	2
1	fennel bulb, diced	1
5 cups	prepared chicken stock (powdered)	1.2 L
2	19 oz/540 ml cans white beans	2
4	14 oz/398 ml cans tomatoes	4
3 tbsp	fresh marjoram, chopped	50 ml
1 tbsp	fresh rosemary, chopped	15 ml
2	fresh sage leaves	2
4 oz	dry bow pasta	125 g
	salt and pepper to taste	

In a large saucepan, heat oil over medium heat. Add garlic, onion, celery, carrots and fennel and sauté, stirring frequently until vegetables are soft.

Add stock and bring to a simmer. Add half the beans, half the tomatoes, 1 tablespoon of marjoram and all the rosemary and sage.

Cover and simmer for 30 minutes. Cook pasta bows, drain and set aside. Remove soup from heat and allow it to cool for 10-15 minutes.

Purée only 3 cups of soup in a blender or food processor and return the purée to the saucepan. Add remaining beans and tomatoes and season with salt and pepper to taste. Add reserved pasta bows and simmer for 2 minutes.

Divide among 6 bowls and garnish with the remaining marjoram.

SERVES: 6   FAT per serving: 4.1 g

Sometimes flatulence is a problem with bean soups. Adding 1/2 tsp of baking soda to the pot may help.

GREEN AND WHITE BEAN SOUP

1 1/2 cups	dried baby lima beans	375 ml
6 cups	water	1.5 L
3	garlic cloves, chopped	3
2 tsp	salt	10 ml
4 cups	prepared beef stock (powdered)	1 L
1/4 tsp	fresh pepper	1 ml
1 tsp	rosemary	5 ml
2 cups	fresh green beans, cut on the diagonal in 1 inch pieces	500 ml
1/2	juice of a lemon	1/2

Wash dried baby lima beans and place them in a large soup pot with the water and bring to a boil. Remove from heat, cover and let stand for one hour.

Return to the heat and simmer, partially covered for half an hour. Mash the garlic with the salt until no large chunks remain. Add to the beans. Add the broth, pepper and rosemary. Simmer until beans are tender.

Cook the fresh green beans in boiling water until they are tender and they look crisp and bright green. Drain and add to the soup when the lima beans are tender but not mushy. Stir in the lemon juice and serve at once, while green beans are bright.

SERVES: 6   FAT per serving: 0.8 g

LENTIL SOUP

3 cups	raw lentils	750 ml
6 cups	prepared vegetable stock (powdered)	1.5 L
2 tsp	salt	10 ml
2 tsp	garlic, minced	10 ml
1 cup	onion, chopped	250 ml
1 cup	celery, minced	250 ml
1 cup	carrots, chopped	250 ml
1/2 cup	tomato juice	125 ml

Sauté onion, carrots, celery and garlic in tomato juice in a large soup pot. Add the vegetable stock and lentils. Bring to a boil and simmer for 1 hour.

Then add:

1 1/2 cups	fresh tomato, chopped	375 ml
2 tbsp	dry red wine	25 ml
2 tbsp	lemon juice	25 ml
1 1/2 tsp	molasses	7 ml
1 tbsp	red wine vinegar	15 ml
1 tsp	thyme	5 ml
1 tsp	oregano	5 ml
	pepper to taste	

Simmer on low for another 20 minutes.

Garnish by sprinkling drops of vinegar and freshly chopped green onions on top of each serving.

SERVES: 8   *FAT per serving: 0.5 g*

LENTIL AND BROWN RICE SOUP

1	envelope of onion or beef soup	1
4 cups	water	1 L
3/4 cups	lentils, rinsed	175 ml
1/2 cup	uncooked brown or white rice	125 ml
1	14 oz / 398 ml can tomatoes, whole, peeled, drained and coarsely chopped	1
1	medium carrot, chopped	1
1	large stalk celery, coarsely chopped	1
1/2 tsp	basil	2 ml
1/2 tsp	oregano	2 ml
1/4 tsp	thyme	1 ml
1 tbsp	parsley, chopped	15 ml
1 tbsp	apple cider vinegar	15 ml
1 tsp	pepper	5 ml

In a large saucepan or stockpot, combine the first 10 ingredients, including the liquid from the tomatoes. Bring to a boil, then simmer, covered, stirring occasionally for 45 minutes or until lentils and rice are tender. Stir in remaining ingredients.

OR

MICROWAVE: In a 3 quart casserole, combine onion soup mix, water, undrained tomatoes, carrot, celery, basil, oregano and thyme.

Heat, covered, on high for 12 minutes or until boiling. Stir in lentils and brown rice and heat, covered, at medium power. Cook for 60 minutes or until lentils are tender. Add parsley, vinegar and pepper. Let stand for 5 minutes before serving.

SERVES: 6   FAT per serving: 0.6 g

Eat bread the way the French and Italians do -
without butter.

SEVEN BEAN SOUP

1 cup	lentils	250 ml
1 cup	yellow split peas	250 ml
1 cup	green split peas	250 ml
1 cup	baby lima beans	250 ml
1 cup	navy beans	250 ml
1 cup	black-eyed peas	250 ml
1 cup	pinto beans	250 ml
12 cups	water	3 L

Rinse all above ingredients and soak overnight in a large soup pot with 12 cups of water.

12 cups	water	3 L
1	bay leaf	1
1/4 cup	chicken broth powder	50 ml
2 cups	onion, chopped	500 ml
1 cup	parsley, chopped	250 ml
1/2 cup	parmesan cheese, grated	125 ml
1 cup	green onion, chopped	250 ml

Drain beans in the morning, add fresh water and the rest of the ingredients, except the green onion and parmesan, which will be used as garnish. Bring to a simmer.

Cover pot and cook until beans are tender, between 2 - 3 hours.

Before serving, mix in the green onion and sprinkle with parmesan cheese.

SERVES: 12   FAT per serving: 1.5 g

Chapter 2

COLD SOUPS

CHILLED BROCCOLI SOUP 18

CHILLED GARDEN SOUP 19

CHILLED GREEK SOUP 20

CHILLED SPANISH GAZPACHO 21

COLD CAULIFLOWER SOUP WITH CURRY 22

COLD YOGURT SOUP WITH FRESH DILL 23

EASY CHILLED AVOCADO SOUP 24

ICED CUCUMBER SOUP 25

ORANGE AND GRAPEFRUIT SOUP 26

VICHYSSOISE SOUP 27

ALL SOUP STOCKS USED IN THIS BOOK ARE MADE FROM POWDERED MIXES BECAUSE THEY ARE LOWER IN FAT.

CHILLED BROCCOLI SOUP

2	bunches broccoli, sliced and chopped	2
1	large onion, sliced	1
2	stalks celery, sliced	2
2 cups	prepared chicken stock (powdered)	500 ml
1/2 cup	cold water	125 ml
3 tbsp	flour	50 ml
1 cup	skim evaporated milk	250 ml
1/2 cup	skim milk yogurt	125 ml
	chives	

Cover and cook in a soup pot, broccoli, onion, celery and chicken stock until mushy. Combine flour and water and gradually stir into vegetable mixture until it comes to a boil.

Purée in blender. Reheat and stir in skim milk. Chill.

Garnish with a dollop of yogurt and chives.

SERVES: 4   FAT per serving: 0.5 g

Did you know that 1 cup of flour = 400 calories but 1 cup of oil = 2000 calories?

CHILLED GARDEN SOUP

16 oz	skim milk yogurt	500 g
1 cup	cucumber purée, peeled and seeded	250 ml
2 tbsp	onion, minced	25 ml
1/4 cup	chili sauce	50 ml
3/4 tsp	salt	3 ml
1 cup	prepared chilled chicken stock	250 ml
	pepper to taste	
1	mild onion, chopped	1
1	green pepper chopped	1
1	English cucumber, chopped	1
1	tomato, chopped	1
	chives	

Blend the first seven ingredients in blender. Chill thoroughly. When ready to serve, mix in vegetables.

Serve in chilled cups and sprinkle with chives.

SERVES: 8   FAT per serving: 0.5 g

You can substitute curry powder for mace.
Add 2 tbsp of lime juice to produce a different taste to the traditional vichyssoise.

CHILLED GREEK SOUP

6 cups	prepared chicken stock (powdered)	1.5 L
1/3 cup	long grain rice	75 ml
1 tsp	salt	5 ml
2	egg whites	2
1	whole egg	1
1/4 cup	lemon juice	50 ml
1 cup	chicken, cooked and shredded, white meat	250 ml
1/4 cup	fresh parsley, chopped	50 ml

Combine stock, rice and salt in a large pot. Bring to a boil. Reduce heat, cover and simmer for 20 minutes.

Beat eggs until frothy. Slowly add lemon juice, beating constantly so eggs don't curdle. Stir a couple of cups of hot broth into eggs, whisking constantly. Gradually pour back into soup. Cook until slightly thickened about 8-10 minutes, stirring frequently. Stir in chicken and parsley.

Cover and refrigerate for several hours. Ladle into bowls and garnish with lemon slices and parsley.

SERVES: 6   FAT per serving: 2.9 g

Broccoli stock is an excellent broth substitute and is very healthy.

CHILLED SPANISH GAZPACHO

1 1/2 tbsp	red wine vinegar	20 ml
2 cups	tomato juice	500 ml
1/2 cup	fresh parsley	125 ml
1/4 cup	green onions, chopped	50 ml
1/2 cup	fresh tomato, chopped	125 ml
1/2 cup	green pepper, chopped	125 ml
1/2 cup	cucumber, chopped	125 ml
1/2 cup	fresh parsley, chopped	125 ml
1	lemon, sliced thin	1

Place tomato juice and vinegar in food processor. With food processor running, add parsley and onions to mince.

Add chopped tomato, green pepper and cucumber to tomato juice mixture and chill one hour.

Serve the gazpacho in chilled bowls, topped with a slice of lemon and fresh parsley.

SERVES: 6   FAT per serving: 0.2 g

There are no "bad" foods, just good food choices.

COLD CAULIFLOWER SOUP WITH CURRY

1/2	cauliflower, cut in chunks	1/2
1 cup	sliced potato, peeled	250 ml
3 1/4 cups	1% milk	800 ml
1 tbsp	soft, light margarine	15 ml
1 tsp	curry powder	5 ml
1 tsp	cumin	5 ml
1 tsp	salt	5 ml
2 tbsp	green onion, chopped	25 ml

In saucepan combine cauliflower, potato and milk. Bring to a boil. Reduce heat, cover and simmer for 20 minutes. Stir in margarine, salt, curry and cumin.

Cover and refrigerate for two hours.

Garnish with green onion and serve chilled.

SERVES: 6   FAT per serving: 2 g

Substitute flavour for fat!

COLD YOGURT SOUP WITH FRESH DILL

This soup can be the star of a happy patio party in the summer.

3/4 cup	yellow raisins	175 ml
4 cups	skim milk yogurt	1 L
1 cup	skim evaporated milk	250 ml
2	medium cucumbers	2
1/2 cup	green onions, finely chopped	125 ml
1/4 cup	fresh dill, chopped	50 ml
8	ice cubes	8
1 tbsp	salt	15 ml
1/2 tsp	white pepper	2 ml
1/4 cup	parsley, finely chopped	50 ml

Soak the raisins in hot water. Set aside. In a soup tureen, mix the yogurt and milk. Peel and half the cucumbers lengthwise, scooping out the seeds. Chop them into 1/4 inch cubes and stir into soup. Add the onions, dill, ice cubes, salt pepper and the drained raisins. Refrigerate for 2-3 hours.

Serve garnished with the parsley.

SERVES: 6-8   FAT per serving: 0.5 g

EASY CHILLED AVOCADO SOUP

Avocados are very high in fat. Half a medium avocado equals 14 grams of fat but used to make 4 servings of soup, it is reasonable.

2 cups	prepared chicken stock (powdered)	500 ml
1	medium avocado	1
1/4 cup	water	50 ml
1 tbsp	lemon juice	15 ml
1/2 cup	light sour cream	125 ml
1/4 cup	artificial bacon bits	50 ml
4	sprigs of parsley	4

Combine chicken stock, avocado, water and lemon juice in blender. Blend until smooth. Add sour cream and further blend until smooth. Chill.

Serve in chilled soup bowls. Sprinkle each serving with bacon bits and a sprig of parsley.

SERVES: 4   FAT per serving: 9.2 g

Cook with olive oil. Olive oil is the main fat in the diet of Mediterranean peoples and may be partially responsible for their lower rates of heart disease. Use it instead of butter, margarine or other vegetable oils in savory dishes.

ICED CUCUMBER SOUP

3	English cucumbers, peeled	3
1	leek, white part only, chopped	1
2	sprays of oil	2
1	bay leaf	1
1 tbsp	flour	15 ml
3 cups	prepared chicken stock (powdered)	750 ml
1 cup	light sour cream	250 ml
	juice of 1/2 lemon	
1 tsp	dill, chopped	5 ml
	salt and pepper to taste	

Chop 2 cucumbers and in a saucepan sauté with leek in oil, on low heat. Stir in the flour. Gradually stir in chicken stock and bay leaf and bring to a boil. Remove the bay leaf. Purée in blender.

Add remaining cucumber, peeled and grated, sour cream and lemon juice. Stir in dill and adjust seasonings with salt and pepper, to taste.

Chill until ready to serve.

SERVES: 6   FAT per serving: 0.8 g

Serving soup in wide bowls adds a lot to the appearance.

ORANGE AND GRAPEFRUIT SOUP

My mother always served fresh fruit to start a meal. Here is a soup that will make a great starter.

1 cup	grapefruit segments	250 ml
1 cup	orange segments	250 ml
3 cups	orange juice	750 ml
1/2 cup	grapefruit juice	125 ml
1/2 cup	lemon juice	125 ml
2 tbsp	plain gelatin	25 ml

Break up the orange and grapefruit segments in a serving bowl and add the orange juice. Mix the other juices with the gelatin in a small saucepan and stir over low heat until the gelatin is dissolved. Add this mixture to the orange and grapefruit segments and chill for at least 2 hours.

This is a refreshing start to a meal but it can also be a fresh desert choice.

SERVES: 6   FAT per serving: 0.3 g

Make your morning café au lait using half strong coffee, half hot skim milk. Sip it from a large bowl for a satisfying, delicious flavour. It is a good source of calcium.

VICHYSSOISE SOUP

This soup may be served hot or cold. It should be served very smooth.

3	medium leeks, finely chopped	3
1	medium onion, finely chopped	1
2	sprays of oil	2
4	medium potatoes, peeled and finely chopped	4
4 cups	prepared chicken stock (powdered)	1 L
1 1/2 cups	skim evaporated milk	375 ml
1/4 tsp	mace	1 ml
1/2 cup	yogurt	125 ml
	salt and white pepper	
	chives, chopped	

Sauté leeks and onion in oil in a saucepan for approximately 3 minutes. Add potatoes and the chicken stock. Simmer until tender, about 15 minutes. Purée in blender.

Add the skim milk, mace, salt and pepper. Remove from heat and, when cool, add yogurt.

Serve in chilled bowl and garnish with chives.

SERVES: 4   FAT per serving: 2.2 g

Peanuts are high in fat, so munch on pretzels instead.

Chapter 3

CREAM SOUPS

CARROT ORANGE CREAM SOUP 30

CREAMY CARROT SOUP 31

CREAMY POTATO AND BROCCOLI SOUP 32

CREAMY SHERRY MUSHROOM BISQUE 33

CREAMY TOMATO SOUP 34

CREOLE PEANUT BUTTER SOUP 35

EASY CREAM OF CORN SOUP 36

PLAIN OLD CREAMY POTATO SOUP 37

ALL SOUP STOCKS USED IN THIS BOOK ARE MADE FROM POWDERED MIXES BECAUSE THEY ARE LOWER IN FAT.

CARROT ORANGE CREAM SOUP

You can serve this soup hot or cold.

2	leeks, chopped white part only	2
1 tbsp	chicken stock powder	15 ml
2 cups	carrots, chopped	500 ml
1 1/2 cups	dry white wine	375 ml
2 tbsp	frozen orange juice concentrate	25 ml
1 tsp	nutmeg	5 ml
2 tsp	curry	10 ml
4 cups	skim evaporated milk	1 L
1	egg white	1
	chopped parsley	

Combine first eight ingredients into a soup pot. Bring to a boil, then simmer gently for one hour, stirring occasionally.

Purée the mixture in a blender. Add the egg white and blend for a few seconds. If the mixture is too thin, thicken with a little flour. If it is too thick, thin by adding more wine.

Pour into cups to serve. Garnish with parsley.

SERVES: 4   FAT per serving: 0.8 g

CREAMY CARROT SOUP

3 cups	water	750 ml
1 tsp	instant chicken stock powder	5 ml
4 1/2 cups	carrots, cut in pieces	1.2 L
1 cup	onion, chopped	250 ml
1/2 cup	celery, chopped	125 ml
1	bay leaf	1
1 tsp	cumin	5 ml
1 1/2 cups	water	375 ml
1 cup	buttermilk	250 ml
1 1/2 tsp	cornstarch mixed with 1/4 cup water	7 ml
2 tsp	parsley, minced	10 ml

Mix water and chicken stock powder in saucepan and bring to a boil. Add carrots, onions, celery and bay leaf to the boiling water. Reduce to simmer and cook until carrots are tender. Remove bay leaf.

Return to soup pot and add cornstarch mixture. Bring to a boil stirring to thicken soup. Remove from heat and add the buttermilk. Do not boil but reheat.

Garnish with parsley.

This soup can be served cold.

SERVES: 12   FAT per serving: 0.5 g

CREAMY POTATO AND BROCCOLI SOUP

1	large potato, peeled and diced	1
1	medium onion, chopped	1
1 1/2 cups	water	375 ml
1 lb	fresh broccoli	500 g
2 tsp	lemon juice	10 ml
1 cup	2% milk	250 ml
1/2 cup	skim milk yogurt	125 ml
	salt and pepper	
	pinch of nutmeg	

In a saucepan, combine potato, onion and water. Cover and cook for 5 - 10 minutes.

Chop broccoli into bite-size pieces. Add to potato mixture and simmer for 5 minutes. Using a slotted spoon, remove a few broccoli florets for garnish.

In blender, purée broccoli - potato mixture and add lemon juice.

Pour in milk and reheat. Season with salt, pepper and nutmeg. Whisk in yogurt before serving.

Garnish each bowl with reserved broccoli florets.

This soup can also be served cold.

SERVES: 6   FAT per serving: 1.1 g

CREAMY SHERRY MUSHROOM BISQUE

1/2 lb	fresh mushrooms	250 g
1 tbsp	margarine	15 ml
3 tbsp	onion, minced	50 ml
2 1/2 tbsp	flour	35 ml
1 cup	prepared hot chicken stock (powdered)	250 ml
1 1/2 cups	2% milk	375 ml
1 tsp	dried tarragon	5 ml
1/4 cup	fresh parsley, chopped	50 ml
2 tbsp	dry sherry	25 ml
	salt and pepper	

Thinly slice mushrooms and set them aside. In a saucepan, sauté margarine and onion until onions are clear. Add sliced mushrooms and cook for 4 minutes. Sprinkle with flour and stir until mixed.

Whisk in hot chicken stock and bring to a boil. Reduce heat and add milk, tarragon, parsley and sherry. Simmer for 4 minutes. Add salt and pepper to taste.

This is a great dish for entertaining. The sherry gives the soup an exotic flavour.

SERVES: 4   FAT per serving: 3.2 g

Defat recipes whenever possible.

CREAMY TOMATO SOUP

2 cups	canned tomatoes	500 ml
1/2 cup	celery, chopped	125 ml
1/2 cup	onion, chopped	125 ml
2 tsp	brown sugar	10 ml
4 cups	skim evaporated milk	1 L
3 tbsp	flour	50 ml
1/2 cup	water	125 ml
	salt and pepper	
	chopped basil	
	skim milk yogurt	

In a heavy pot, simmer tomatoes, celery, onion and brown sugar. Then purée mixture in blender. Add purée mixture with the canned, skim milk. Reheat and slowly add flour mixed with water to the mixture and stir until thick. Season with salt and pepper.

Serve in heated bowls garnished with basil and a dollop of skim milk yogurt.

SERVES: 4   FAT per serving: 1.2 g

Perk up your day with fresh-from-the-oven low fat muffins.

CREOLE PEANUT BUTTER SOUP

For the peanut butter lover!

2	sprays of oil	2
1	medium sized onion, peeled and sliced	1
1 tbsp	flour	15 ml
1 1/2 tsp	salt	7 ml
1/2 tsp	celery salt	2 ml
2 tbsp	light peanut butter	25 ml
2 cups	skim evaporated milk	500 ml
2 cups	tomato juice	500 ml
3 tbsp	fresh parsley, chopped	50 ml

Spray pot with oil and sauté onion on medium heat. Stir in flour and seasonings. Mix in peanut butter and milk. Continue to cook over medium heat, stirring constantly, until thick and smooth.

Add tomato juice and bring to a boil. Sprinkle with parsley and serve.

SERVES: 4   FAT per serving: 3.5 g

Fried chicken is the dickens.

EASY CREAM OF CORN SOUP

2 1/2 cups	cream style corn	625 ml
2	sprays of vegetable oil	2
1/2	medium onion, sliced	1/2
3 tbsp	flour, mixed with water	50 ml
1 1/2 tsp	salt	7 ml
1/2 tsp	white pepper	2 ml
1/2 tsp	nutmeg	2 ml
3 cups	skim milk	750 ml

Purée corn and set it aside. Sauté onion until clear. Stir in flour, salt, pepper and nutmeg. Stir in corn. Purée this mixture and add milk.

Heat and serve soup sprinkled with parsley.

SERVES: 4   FAT per serving: 0.8 g

Make fruit your everyday desert, saving rich sweets for a special occasion.

PLAIN OLD CREAMY POTATO SOUP

1	small onion, chopped	250 ml
1 cup	celery, chopped	250 ml
2 cups	potatoes, peeled and sliced	500 ml
1 1/2 tsp	salt	7 ml
1 cup	water	250 ml
2 cups	skim evaporated milk	500 ml
1/4 tsp	dried parsley	1 ml
	white pepper	

Place first five ingredients in saucepan. Cover and boil until potatoes are done. Pour in milk, pepper and parsley. Purée soup in blender and reheat.

Serve in wide bowls garnished with a sprig of parsley.

SERVES: 4   FAT per serving: 0.5 g

Did you know that 2 Tbsp of peanut butter = 16 grams of fat.

Chapter 4

MEAT SOUPS

ANGEL-HAIR SOUP 40

CHICKEN VEGETABLE SOUP WITH CURRY 42

HUNGARIAN BEEF GOULASH SOUP 44

ITALIAN CHICK-PEA SAUSAGE SOUP 46

LAMB SOUP STEW 48

LEFT-OVER TURKEY SOUP 49

MULLIGATAWNY SOUP 50

MIDDLE EASTERN CHICKEN SOUP 52

TURKEY MEATBALL SOUP 53

TURKEY CREOLE JAMBALAYA 54

ALL SOUP STOCKS USED IN THIS BOOK ARE MADE FROM POWDERED MIXES BECAUSE THEY ARE LOWER IN FAT.

ANGEL-HAIR SOUP

2 tbsp	soy sauce	25 ml
1 tbsp	red wine vinegar	15 ml
1 tsp	fresh ginger	5 ml
1 tsp	tomato paste	5 ml
1	clove garlic, minced	1
6 oz	pork tenderloin	175 g
1	leek, white and light green parts	1
5 cups	prepared chicken stock (powdered)	1.2 L
1/2 cup	cilantro, chopped	125 ml
2	celery stalks, cut on the diagonal, into 1/4 inch slices	2
4 oz	snow peas	125 g
2	carrots, peeled and cut on the diagonal, into 1/4 inch slices	2
1 cup	bean sprouts	250 ml
4 oz	dry angel hair pasta	125 g
	salt and pepper to taste	

In a small bowl, whisk together soy sauce, vinegar, ginger, tomato paste and garlic. Marinate the pork in this mixture for 1-4 hours. Remove the pork and strain the marinate.

Sauté the pork for about 3 minutes on each side. Slice thinly and set aside.

Clean and slice leek. Set aside. Combine stock, cilantro and leek in a large saucepan and bring to a simmer over medium-low heat.

Blanch celery, snow peas and carrots. Set aside. Add angel hair to stock mixture and boil for 3 minutes. Remove from heat and add celery, snow peas, carrots and bean sprouts.

Serve immediately in bowls and garnish with pork slices.

SERVES: 4   FAT per serving: 2.4 g

Mirepoix is a mixture of rough cut carrots, onions and celery. Many soups are started by sautéeing a mirepoix.

CHICKEN VEGETABLE SOUP WITH CURRY

2 tsp	vegetable oil	10 ml
1 cup	onion, chopped	250 ml
2 tsp	garlic, minced	10 ml
2 tsp	fresh ginger, minced	10 ml
2 tsp	curry powder	10 ml
1 tsp	chicken broth powder	5 ml
1 tsp	turmeric	5 ml
1/2 cup	tomato paste	125 ml
1 1/2 cups	water	375 ml
2 cups	broccoli florets	500 ml
2 cups	carrots, sliced thin	500 ml
3 cups	cauliflower, cut	750 ml
3 cups	skim milk	750 ml
1/4 cup	cornstarch	50 ml
1/2 cup	skim milk	125 ml
1/2 lb	chicken, cooked and shredded	250 g
1/2 cup	skim milk yogurt	125 ml
2 tsp	green onion tops	10 ml

Heat oil in soup pot and sauté onion, garlic and ginger until tender. Add curry powder, broth powder and turmeric to onion mixture.

Add tomato paste and water to pot and bring to a boil. Add to pot the broccoli, carrots, cauliflower and milk. Simmer for 30 minutes. Combine cornstarch and 1/2 cup skim milk and whisk into soup to thicken. Add chicken to soup and reheat.

Serve with a dollop of yogurt and green onion tops.

SERVES: 12   FAT per serving: 2.5 g

Substitute apple juice for chicken broth and curry powder for mace.

HUNGARIAN BEEF GOULASH SOUP

2 cups	inside round steak, chopped in 1 inch pieces, trimmed of visible fat	500 ml
2	sprays of vegetable oil	2
2	medium onions, chopped	2
3	garlic cloves, minced	3
2 tsp	salt	10 ml
1/8 tsp	cayenne pepper	.5 ml
3 tbsp	paprika	50 ml
1 tsp	caraway seeds	5 ml
4 cups	hot water	1 L
1	19 oz can tomatoes, undrained, crushed	630 ml
4-6	medium potatoes, cut in 3/4 inch cubes	4-6
2	medium green peppers, seeded and coarsely chopped	2
1 cup	skim milk yogurt	250 ml

Dry beef with a paper towel. Heat oil in a heavy saucepan and add the beef. Cook, stirring on medium heat until the pieces lose their colour. Add the onions and garlic and continue cooking until onions have softened but not browned.

Stir in the salt, cayenne, paprika and caraway seeds. Pour in the water and bring to a boil. Reduce heat and simmer, partially covered for half an hour. Add the tomatoes, continue to simmer, partially covered, for another half to three quarters of an hour until meat is tender. Add the potatoes and green pepper. Cover and simmer 20 to 30 minutes until potatoes are cooked and meat is tender.

Serve in large bowls; offer yogurt separately.

SERVES: 6   FAT per serving: 5 g

To reduce fat even more, use canned evaporated skim milk. It has a thick consistency.

ITALIAN CHICK-PEA SAUSAGE SOUP

This soup is rather high in fat so make it your main meal of the day.

2	sprays of oil	2
1 cup	sliced hot Italian sausage, cooked	250 ml
1	onion, chopped	1
1 tbsp	garlic, minced	15 ml
1	tomato, chopped	1
1 tbsp	tomato paste	15 ml
1 cup	cooked or canned chick-peas	250 ml
3 cups	vegetable stock	750 ml
3/4 cup	small pasta, eg. elbow	175 ml
1 1/2 tsp	dried basil	7 ml
1/2 tsp	rosemary	2 ml
1/4 cup	fresh parsley, chopped salt and pepper	50 ml
1/4 cup	freshly grated parmesan cheese	50 ml

In large saucepan heat oil over medium heat. Cook sausage and set aside, draining it on paper towels.

Cook onion and garlic until softened. Stir in tomato and tomato paste. Cook for a minute. Add chick-peas and vegetable stock and bring to a boil.

Add pasta, basil, sausage and rosemary. Reduce heat and simmer for 10 to 15 minutes or until pasta is tender, yet firm. Add parsley, salt and pepper to taste.

Sprinkle each bowl with parmesan cheese.

SERVES: 4   FAT per serving: 19.9 g

Instant mashed potatoes are great in homemade bread - they keep moisture in. Substitute the potatoes for fat.

LAMB SOUP STEW

1 lb	boneless lamb shoulder, cut in 1 inch cubes, fat trimmed off	500 g
2	sprays of oil	2
1	small onion, sliced	1
3 cups	prepared beef stock (powdered)	750 ml
2 cups	prepared chicken stock (powdered)	500 ml
2	sprigs parsley	2
1 tsp	salt	5 ml
1/4 tsp	pepper	1 ml
1	bay leaf	1
1 tsp	paprika	5 ml
1/2 tsp	rosemary leaves	2 ml
1/4 tsp	thyme leaves	1 ml
1/4 cup	pearl barley	50 ml
2	medium carrots, sliced	2
2	10 oz pkg. frozen brussel sprouts, thawed and halved	2
1/4 lb	mushrooms, sliced	125 g

Spray oil in bottom of Dutch oven. Heat to medium and brown the lamb. Add the onion and sauté for 2 minutes. Add the stock, parsley and seasonings.

Simmer covered for 30 minutes. Stir in barley and cook 30 minutes longer. Discard bay leaf and parsley. Add vegetables, cook 20 minutes or until vegetables and meat are tender.

SERVES: 4   FAT per serving: 11.7 g

LEFT-OVER TURKEY SOUP

This is a great recipe to stretch your Thanksgiving or Christmas turkey.

12 cups	water	3 L
1	turkey carcass, pull off meat and reserve	1
1	bay leaf	1
2 cups	celery, sliced	500 ml
1 cup	onion, diced	250 ml
1/4 cup	instant mashed potato flakes	50 ml
3 cups	turkey meat, pulled from carcass	750 ml
2 1/2 cups	fresh mushrooms, sliced	625 ml
1/2 cup	fresh parsley	125 ml

Combine in soup pot, the turkey carcass, water and bay leaves and simmer for 3 - 4 hours.

Cool and refrigerate. Skim the hardened fat and remove bones, skin and bay leaves.

Add celery and onion and simmer for 15 minutes. Stir potato flakes into soup, beating and stirring to thicken broth. Add mushrooms, turkey meat and simmer another 10 minutes.

Garnish with parsley.

For a thicker soup, add more potato flakes.

SERVES: 12   FAT per serving: 3.7 g

MULLIGATAWNY SOUP

This chicken soup-stew probably got into western cuisine from India. The name actually means "pepper water".

3	sprays of vegetable oil	3
2 lbs	skinless chicken (white meat)	1 kg
1	medium onion, finely chopped	1
1	medium green pepper, chopped	1
2	celery sticks, chopped	2
1	medium green apple, finely chopped	1
1 1/2 tsp	salt	7 ml
1/8 tsp	each of ground cloves and cayenne	.5 ml
2 tbsp	flour	25 ml
1 tbsp	curry powder	15 ml
6 cups	chicken broth	1.5 L
3 cups	hot, boiled rice	750 ml
1/4 cup	parsley, chopped	50 ml
	juice of 1 lemon	

Heat oil sprays in a soup pot and lightly brown the chicken on medium heat. Add the onion, green pepper, celery and apple. Stir in salt, cloves and cayenne. Stir and cook until onions are slightly soft. Sprinkle flour and curry over all and mix well.

Pour chicken broth in gradually, stirring to clear the bottom of the pan. Bring to a boil, reduce heat and simmer covered for 45-60 minutes. Stir in lemon juice.

Serve the soup in large bowls with a mound of hot rice in the middle. Sprinkle parsley over all.

SERVES: 6   FAT per serving: 10 g

My mission is healthy eating and creative cooking.

MIDDLE EASTERN CHICKEN SOUP

Mint and yogurt gives this rather sturdy rice and chicken soup a lovely lightness.

2	sprays of vegetable oil	2
10	green onions with crisp tops, chopped	10
1/2 tsp	thyme	2 ml
2 tsp	dried mint, crumbled	10 ml
1 1/4 tsp	salt	6 ml
1/4 tsp	white pepper	1 ml
6 cups	vegetable broth	1.5 L
1/4 cup	rice	50 ml
3 cups	cooked chicken, white meat, cubed	750 ml
1 cup	skim-milk yogurt	250 ml
1/4 cup	fresh dill, chopped	50 ml

Heat the oil in a saucepan on medium heat and add the green onions. Stir in the thyme, mint, salt and pepper and broth. Bring to a boil, stir in the rice. Cover, reduce heat and simmer for 15-20 minutes.

Add the chicken and cook for 3 minutes. Put the yogurt in a small bowl and carefully stir in a few tablespoons of the hot soup to make a smooth mixture. Add the yogurt mixture to the soup, taste and add salt if needed. Heat gently but do not let it boil.

Serve sprinkled with fresh dill.

SERVES: 6   FAT per serving: 3.5 g

TURKEY MEATBALL SOUP

6 oz	lean ground turkey	175 g
2	cloves garlic, minced	2
1	egg white, beaten	1
3 tbsp	dry bead crumbs	50 ml
1 cup	flat leaf parsley, chopped	250 ml
1 tsp	salt	5 ml
1/4 tsp	freshly ground pepper	1 ml
6 cups	chicken stock	1.5 L
1	medium onion, diced	1
2	medium carrots, sliced on the diagonal	2
1 cup	dry elbow pasta	250 ml

In a medium bowl, combine turkey, garlic, egg white, bread crumbs, 1/2 cup parsley, salt and pepper. Mix well with your hands. Using a scoop, form 1 inch meatballs and refrigerate until ready to use.

In a large saucepan, heat 3 tbsp of stock over medium heat. Add onion and sauté. Add carrots and remaining stock and bring to a boil. Add pasta and cook for another 5 minutes.

Lower heat and add the meatballs and simmer for about 10 minutes. Remove from heat and stir in remaining parsley. Season with salt and pepper.

SERVES: 4   FAT per serving: 9.2 g

TURKEY CREOLE JAMBALAYA

Traditionally, ham or sausage is used in this New Orleans dish but in this recipe I have substituted ground turkey because it is much lower in fat.

1 lb	ground turkey (lean)	500 g
2 tbsp	cooking oil	25 ml
2 tbsp	flour	25 ml
2	medium onions, chopped	2
3	garlic cloves, minced	3
2	medium green peppers, chopped	2
1	medium red pepper, chopped	1
2	celery sticks, chopped	2
1	bay leaf	1
1 1/2 tsp	thyme	7 ml
1/4 tsp	cayenne	1 ml
1 tbsp	salt	15 ml
2 cups	canned tomatoes, crushed	500 ml
3 cups	water	750 ml
2 cups	uncooked rice	500 ml
1 lb	fresh or frozen shrimp, shelled and drained	500 g
1/2 cup	parsley, chopped	125 ml
1/2 cup	green onion, chopped	125 ml

Sauté the turkey in a large skillet. Set aside on paper towels to drain. In a heavy saucepan, make a smooth mixture of the oil and flour. Stir over moderate heat until mixture is a rich, nutty or butterscotch brown and is creamy in texture. This takes about 10 minutes or more of careful attention.

Add the onions, garlic, peppers and celery. Stir and cook until onions are slightly soft but not brown. Add the bay leaf, thyme, cayenne, salt, tomatoes and water. Bring to a boil and add the ground turkey. Cover and simmer for 15 minutes.

Add rice, bring to a boil again, stir once and cover. Reduce heat and simmer for 25-30 minutes or until rice is cooked. Carefully stir in shrimp. Simmer another 3-5 minutes. Remove the bay leaf.

Stir the mixture of parsley and green onions onto the top of the jambalaya.

SERVES: 8   FAT per serving: 12 g

8 oz (250 ml) of whole milk = 9 g of fat; 2% milk = 5 g; 1% milk = 2.5 g; skim milk = 0 g; 1/2 cup canned evaporated skim milk = 0.4 g.

Chapter 5

PURÉED SOUPS

ASPARAGUS SOUP 58

HALLOWE'EN PUMPKIN SOUP 59

HENRY'S CREAMY BORSCHT 60

NO FAT QUICK BLENDER SOUP 61

OLD FASHIONED SPLIT PEA SOUP 62

PARSNIP SOUP WITH GINGER 63

PEAR SOUP 64

POTATO PICK-ME-UP BROTH 65

SPINACH SOUP 66

SPINACH OYSTER PUREE SOUP 67

SWEET RED PEPPER SOUP 68

TOMATO SOUP CARIBBEAN STYLE 69

YELLOW SQUASH SOUP 70

ALL SOUP STOCKS USED IN THIS BOOK ARE MADE FROM POWDERED MIXES BECAUSE THEY ARE LOWER IN FAT.

ASPARAGUS SOUP

1	bunch asparagus, (10 sprigs)	1
1	onion, chopped	1
2 cups	potatoes, peeled and diced	2
1	clove garlic, minced	1
1 1/2 cups	water	375 ml
1/2 tsp	thyme	2 ml
1/4 tsp	pepper	1 ml
1/4 tsp	nutmeg	1 ml
1 1/2 cups	skim evaporated milk	375 ml
	salt to taste	

Peel asparagus stems and break off hard bottoms. Coarsely chop stems and set them aside. Reserve asparagus tips. In a sauce pan, combine chopped asparagus stems, onions, potatoes, garlic, water, thyme, pepper and nutmeg. Bring to a boil.

Reduce heat, cover and simmer for 10 minutes or until potatoes are done. In the meantime, steam reserved asparagus tips for 3 minutes.

In a blender, purée soup in batches until smooth and return to pot. Add skim milk, heat through but do not boil.

Season with salt and pepper.

Divide asparagus tips among 5 bowls; pour soup into bowls.

SERVES: 5   FAT per serving: 0.5 g

HALLOWE'EN PUMPKIN SOUP

4 cups	pumpkin, peeled and cubed	1 L
2	medium potatoes, peeled and cubed	2
1	large onion, sliced	1
2 cups	prepared chicken stock (powdered)	500 ml
2 tbsp	vegetable oil	25 ml
2 tbsp	fresh parsley, chopped	25 ml
2	cloves garlic, minced	2
3/4 cup	skim evaporated milk	175 ml
1 tsp	dried basil	5 ml
	fresh mint leaves, chopped	

In a large pot, combine pumpkin, potatoes, onion and chicken stock, oil, parsley and garlic. Cover and simmer for 45 minutes, stirring occasionally.

In blender, purée mixture. Return to pot, add milk and basil and heat until hot.

Garnish each serving with mint leaves.

SERVES: 8   FAT per serving: 4.1 g

Eat less, more often.

HENRY'S CREAMY BORSCHT

This recipe is quick and so easy!

1	large white onion, coarsely chopped	1	
1	clove garlic, crushed	1	
3	14 oz/398 ml cans sliced beets	3	
1 cup	chicken stock	250 ml	
1 tsp	dill, dried or fresh	5 ml	
1 cup	cucumber, peeled and chopped	250 ml	
1 qt	light buttermilk	1 L	
	salt and pepper to taste		
	low fat sour cream		
1/4 cup	chives	50 ml	

In a soup pot, on medium heat, sauté onion and garlic with a tablespoon of water.

Add beets, chicken stock and dill. Simmer for 30 minutes. Add cucumber.

Purée in blender and add buttermilk. Season to taste.

Reheat and serve, do not boil.

Garnish with a dollop of sour cream and sprinkle of chives.

SERVES: 6   FAT per serving: 1.8 g

If you want less fat on you, put less fat in you.

NO FAT QUICK BLENDER SOUP

3 cups	water	750 ml
1/4 cup	cornstarch, powdered	50 ml
2 cups	mixed vegetables, coarsely cut	500 ml
	salt and pepper to taste	

Heat all vegetables until they are tender. Mix the cornstarch and water and bring to a boil. Add the mixture to the vegetables. Season with salt and pepper. Purée in blender. Reheat and serve.

SERVES: 4   FAT per serving: trace

Substitute skim milk yogurt for butter, oil and margarine whenever possible.

OLD FASHIONED SPLIT PEA SOUP

1 1/2 cups	green split peas	375 ml
8 cups	hot chicken stock	2 L
1 cup	celery, chopped	250 ml
1 cup	carrot, chopped	250 ml
1/2 cup	onion, chopped	125 ml
1/2 tsp	thyme	2 ml
1/2 tsp	sage	2 ml
2	bay leaves	2
1/4 tsp	hot sauce	1 ml

Combine all ingredients in soup pot and bring to a boil. Reduce to simmer and cook for one hour. Cool soup, remove bay leaves and purée in blender.

Season to taste with salt and pepper. Reheat and serve.

SERVES: 10   FAT per serving: 1 g

The true, natural flavour of vegetables comes through without added fat.

PARSNIP SOUP WITH GINGER

1	onion, chopped	1
4	medium parsnips, peeled and cubed	4
1 cup	water	250 ml
1 tbsp	light margarine	15 ml
1 tbsp	all purpose flour	15 ml
1 cup	chicken stock	250 ml
1 1/2 tsp	fresh ginger root, grated	7 ml
3/4 cup	2% milk	175 ml
	salt and pepper	

In saucepan combine onion, parsnips and water. Simmer covered for 8 to 10 minutes or until parsnips are tender. Purée in blender.

In saucepan melt soft margarine over medium heat. Stir in flour and cook for 1 minute.

Stir in chicken stock and cook until mixture thickens. Add puréed parsnip mixture, ginger root, milk and salt and pepper to taste. Heat through and serve.

SERVES: 5   FAT per serving: 2 g

Buy non-stick pans to reduce the amount of oil needed to cook.

PEAR SOUP

This is a different but pleasant change of pace.

3	sprays of oil	3
1	large onion, chopped	1
1/2 tsp	curry powder	2 ml
4	ripe pears	4
3 cups	prepared vegetable stock (powdered)	750 ml
1 1/2 tsp	lemon juice	7 ml

Heat oil sprays in a large saucepan. Add onion and sprinkle with curry powder. Sauté until onion is soft.

Peel, quarter and core pears. Chop and add to onion. Add vegetable stock and lemon juice and bring to a boil.

Simmer until pears are tender. Purée in blender.

Serve hot with a wedge of lemon.

SERVES: 4   FAT per serving: 1.7 g

Use oil sprays on pans to reduce the fat.

POTATO PICK-ME-UP BROTH

3/4 cup	potato, chopped and peeled	175 ml
2 1/2 cups	fresh vegetables (carrot, celery, peas, broccoli, bok choy etc.)	625 ml
2 1/2 cups	water	625 ml
1 tsp	vegetable stock powder	5 ml

Cook all vegetables until tender. Cool and purée in blender. Add vegetable stock mix (powder) for seasoning.

SERVES: 4   FAT per serving: 0.4 g

Get more protein from plant sources like grains, legumes, nuts and seeds.

SPINACH SOUP

2 lbs	tender young spinach or 2 packages of frozen spinach	1 kg
2	sprays of vegetable oil	2
1/4 cup	onion, minced	50 ml
4 cups	prepared vegetable stock (powdered)	1 L
1/2 tsp	nutmeg	2 ml
1/2 tsp	paprika	2 ml
	salt and pepper to taste	
	skim milk yogurt	

Sauté spinach with onion in a hot pot sprayed with oil. Purée spinach in blender. Return to pot and add the vegetable stock, nutmeg, paprika, salt and pepper.

Bring soup slowly to a boil and serve.

Garnish with a dollop of yogurt.

SERVES: 6   FAT per serving: 0.4 g

Trap fat from soups and stews with a strainer.

SPINACH OYSTER PUREE SOUP

2 cups	1% milk	500 ml
20	oysters, blanched and puréed	20
1/4 cup	spinach, cooked and puréed	50 ml
2 tbsp	cornstarch	25 ml
1 cup	skim evaporated milk	250 ml
1 tsp	A-1 sauce	5 ml
	dash of garlic salt	
	salt and pepper to taste	
	grated lemon rind	

Heat milk. Add oysters and spinach purées. Bring to a simmering point but do not let boil.

Thicken with cornstarch mixed with cold water. Simmer several minutes to allow cornstarch to cook. Add the milk and seasonings.

Garnish with grated lemon.

SERVES: 4   FAT per serving: 2.9 g

SWEET RED PEPPER SOUP

2	sprays of vegetable oil	2
1 cup	onion, chopped	250 ml
1	large potato, peeled and chopped	1
6 cups	prepared vegetable stock (powdered)	1.5 L
2	fresh thyme sprigs	2
2	bay leaves	2
4	large red peppers, seeded and chopped	4
	salt and pepper	

Heat oil sprays in a heavy pot. Sauté the onion on medium heat until soft. Add the potato and vegetable stock and boil for 15 minutes.

Reduce heat. Add the thyme and bay leaves and the red peppers. Cook for about 45 minutes. Remove bay leaf. Transfer soup to a blender and purée until smooth. Reheat and serve.

SERVES: 4   FAT per serving: 0.6 g

If soup is homemade, sodium content is greatly reduced.

TOMATO SOUP CARIBBEAN STYLE

2 1/2 cups	tomato juice	625 ml
1/2 cup	carrot, grated	125 ml
1/4 cup	celery, finely chopped	50 ml
3 tbsp	green onion, finely chopped	50 ml
2 tbsp	green pepper, finely chopped	25 ml
2 tbsp	fresh basil, finely chopped	25 ml
1/2 tsp	fresh pepper, freshly ground	2 ml
1/4 tsp	honey	1 ml
1/3 cup	buttermilk	75 ml
2 tbsp	fresh parsley, finely chopped	25 ml

Simmer tomato juice in saucepan. Add carrot, celery, onion, green pepper, basil and honey and simmer for 30 minutes. Add buttermilk to soup. Do not boil.

Serve in bowls garnished with fresh parsley.

If you want a thicker soup, purée the mixture.

SERVES: 6   FAT per serving: trace

Try apple juice instead of chicken stock as the base for a soup.

YELLOW SQUASH SOUP

1 1/2 cups	any type of yellow squash, chopped into small pieces	375 ml
1/2 cup	onion, chopped	125 ml
1/4 cup	yellow bell pepper, chopped	50 ml
1 1/2 cups	prepared vegetable stock (powdered)	375 ml
1/2 tsp	cumin	2 ml
1/2 tsp	curry	2 ml
1 tsp	nutmeg	5 ml
1 tsp	salt	5 ml
1/2 tsp	pepper	2 ml
2 tbsp	skim milk yogurt	25 ml
2 tsp	parsley flakes	10 ml

Peel, chop and place squash in saucepan. Add onion, pepper, vegetable stock, and cook until vegetables are tender. Cool, place in blender and process until smooth.

Add to blender contents cumin, curry, nutmeg, salt and pepper. Return to pot to heat.

Garnish each bowl with a teaspoon of yogurt and sprinkle of parsley.

SERVES: 4　　　　　　　　　　　　　　　FAT per serving: trace

Chapter 6

SEAFOOD & FISH SOUPS

CURRIED FISH SOUP 72

CRAB MEAT SOUP WITH SAVORY 74

FISH CHOWDER 75

JAPANESE NOODLE SOUP 76

OYSTER AND CLAM CHOWDER 77

RUSSIAN PINK SALMON SOUP 78

SAN FRANCISCO FISH SOUP 79

SCALLOP AND FENNEL NOODLE SOUP 80

TOMATO CLAM SOUP 82

YUMMY CLAM CHOWDER 83

ALL SOUP STOCKS USED IN THIS BOOK ARE MADE FROM POWDERED MIXES BECAUSE THEY ARE LOWER IN FAT.

CURRIED FISH SOUP

1 tbsp	butter or light margarine	15 ml
1	small onion, finely chopped	1
2	garlic cloves, minced	2
1	tart apple, peeled, cored, finely chopped	1
2 tbsp	curry powder	25 ml
2 tsp	cumin	10 ml
2 tbsp	flour	25 ml
1 cup	dry white wine	250 ml
3 cups	water	750 ml
2 cups	clams, including broth	500 ml
1 tsp	salt	5 ml
1/4 cup	rice	50 ml
1 lb	fish fillets such as monk or cod	500 g
1/2 lb	scallops, cut in half	250 g
1/2 cup	skim evaporated milk	125 ml
1/2 cup	parsley, finely chopped	125 ml

In a heavy, wide saucepan that has a lid, melt the butter or margarine. Add the onion, garlic and apple and cook on low heat until onions soften. Stir in the curry powder, cumin and flour. Add the wine, stirring with a whisk. Bring to a simmer.

Add the water, clams and salt and bring to a boil. Then return to a simmer. Cook on very low heat, partially covered for 45 minutes, stirring occasionally.

If some liquid cooks away, replace it with water. Turn up the heat and stir in the rice. Cover lightly and cook on low heat again for 15-20 minutes. Cut fish fillets across at 2 inch intervals and add them to the pot. Cover and cook about 4 minutes or until fish is opaque. Put in the scallops, cover and cook for 1-2 minutes. Stir in milk and serve the soup in large, hot bowls or on soup plates. Sprinkle with parsley.

SERVES: 4   FAT per serving: 3.2 g

Make carbohydrates - like pasta - your main dish.
It's very filling and healthy.

CRAB MEAT SOUP WITH SAVORY

2/3 cups	brown rice	150 ml
1/2 tsp	savory	2 ml
1 1/3 cups	water	325 ml
4 cups	prepared chicken stock (powdered)	1 L
1 cup	crab meat, shredded	250 ml
2 tbsp	fresh parsley	25 ml

Bring water to a boil. Add rice and savory. Cover and heat on low for one hour.

Add chicken stock and crab meat to cooked rice. Heat and serve.

Garnish with fresh parsley.

This is a great way to use left over crab and rice.

SERVES: 6   FAT per serving: 1.8 g

Fat so often masks great natural flavours.

FISH CHOWDER

1 tbsp	butter	15 ml
1	onion, finely chopped	1
1	carrot, finely chopped	1
1	celery stick, finely chopped	1
4	potatoes, diced	4
2 cups	water	500 ml
2 cups	skim evaporated milk	500 ml
1 lb	monk fish or other, fresh or frozen	500 g
1 cup	kernel corn	250 ml
1 tsp	salt	5 ml
1/2 tsp	fresh ground pepper	2 ml
	chopped fresh parsley	

In heavy saucepan melt butter. Add onion, carrot, celery and potatoes and cook over medium heat, stirring occasionally for five minutes. Add water, cover and simmer until vegetables are tender. Stir in milk, fish chunks and corn. Simmer for 5 to 10 minutes.

Add salt and pepper to taste and garnish with chopped parsley.

Any fresh or frozen fillets can be used but try monk fish if it is available.

SERVES: 6 - 1 cup   FAT per serving: 3 g

JAPANESE NOODLE SOUP

1 tsp	sesame oil	5 ml
1 tsp	fresh ginger, minced	5 ml
2	garlic cloves, minced	2
1	green pepper, cut in thin strips	1
1 tbsp	soy sauce	15 ml
4 cups	prepared chicken stock (powdered)	1 L
1/2 lb	fine Japanese noodles, cooked and drained	250 g
1/2 lb	shrimp, cooked	250 g
2	green onions, chopped	2

Heat the oil in a heavy saucepan. Add the ginger and garlic. Stir briefly, not long enough to brown. Add the green pepper strips. Stir and cook for 30 seconds. Add the soy sauce and chicken broth. Stir and bring to a boil.

Add the noodles, cooked, according to the package directions. When the noodles are hot, add the shrimp just to warm.

Serve sprinkled with chopped green onions.

SERVES: 4   FAT per serving: 4.1 g

OYSTER AND CLAM CHOWDER

This is a thick soup, a meal in itself!

2	sprays of oil	2
1 cup	celery, diced	250 ml
2	carrots, shredded	2
6	green onions, chopped	6
1	medium leek, sliced	1
1/2 cup	flour	125 ml
4 cups	1% milk	1 L
1	10 oz / 284 ml can clams, minced	1
2 cups	oysters, canned or fresh	500 ml
1/2 cup	white wine	125 ml

Combine first 5 ingredients in soup pot and sauté on medium heat. Add flour and mix. Slowly stir in milk. Add clams, oysters and wine and stir over low heat for 10 minutes. Do not boil. Serve hot.

SERVES: 4   FAT per serving: 4.3 g

Hungry? Try having 2 baked potatoes with low fat sour cream and chopped chives.

RUSSIAN PINK SALMON SOUP

This soup is so good looking — pink salmon in a broth coloured faintly by the tomatoes, garnished with green and black olives and lemon slices.

1 tbsp	olive oil	15 ml
3	large tomatoes, peeled, seeded and chopped	3
2	medium onions, chopped	2
2	large dill pickles, finely chopped	2
6	green olives, pitted	6
6	black olives, pitted	6
1 tsp	capers, drained	5 ml
2 qt	prepared fish stock (powdered)	2 L
1	bay leaf	1
2	sprigs parsley	2
	salt and pepper	
1 lb	salmon, cut in two strips	500 g
	lemon slices	

Put oil in a large saucepan. Add the tomatoes and cook slowly, stirring until paste is formed. Add the onions and pickles. Chop 2 green olives and 2 black olives and add them with the capers. Stir to mix. Pour in the stock gradually, stirring. Add the bay leaf, parsley, salt and pepper to taste. Bring to a simmer and heat for 10 minutes. Put in the salmon and cook for 3-5 minutes or until salmon is just done. Pick out and discard the bay leaf and parsley.

Slice the remaining olives and strew over the soup. Garnish with lemon slices.

SERVES: 4   FAT per serving: 12.5 g

SAN FRANCISCO FISH SOUP

2	sprays of oil	2
1	medium onion, finely chopped	1
3	cloves garlic, minced	3
3 cups	dry white wine, separated	750 ml
1	medium green pepper, coarsely chopped	1
2 lbs	fresh tomatoes, peeled, seeded, chopped	1 kg
3 oz	tomato paste	90 g
1 tsp	freshly ground pepper	5 ml
1 tsp	dried oregano	5 ml
2 tbsp	fresh basil, finely chopped	25 ml
2 lbs	fresh white-flesh fish	1 kg
3/4 lb	scallops	375 g
3/4 lb	raw shrimp	375 g
1 1/2 lb	mock crab	750 g
1	4 oz / 142 ml can clams	1
	fresh parsley, chopped	

In a large soup pot heat the oil and add the onion, garlic, 1 cup of wine and green pepper. Sauté over medium heat until vegetables start to soften. Add the tomatoes, tomato paste, remaining wine, pepper, herbs and juice from canned clams. Simmer for 20 minutes.

Add the fish, scallops, shrimp and crab. Simmer for about 5 minutes. Do not stir. Add the clams and heat for a scant 1 minute. Sprinkle with parsley.

SERVES: 8   FAT per serving: 4.7 g

SCALLOP AND FENNEL NOODLE SOUP

2 tbsp	sherry	25 ml
1 tbsp	lemon juice	15 ml
2 tbsp	light soy sauce	25 ml
1	garlic clove, minced	1
1/2	fresh jalapeno pepper, minced	1/2
1 tsp	fresh ginger, minced	5 ml
1 tsp	cumin	5 ml
16	raw scallops	16
4 oz	linguini - rice noodles	125 g
2	drops sesame oil	2
1	medium onion, sliced thin	1
1	fennel bulb, cored and sliced thin	1
5 cups	prepared chicken stock (powdered)	1.2 L
1 cup	Chinese cabbage, sliced thin	250 ml
1	red bell pepper, sliced in 1/4 inch strips	1
2 tbsp	fresh chives	25 ml

In a small bowl, whisk together the first seven ingredients. Add the scallops and marinate for 30 minutes.

Cook linguini el dente. Drain and set aside.

In a large skillet, heat the sesame oil over medium heat. Add the onion and fennel and stir fry until they begin to wilt. Add scallops and marinate and stir fry until scallops are done, about 2-3 minutes.

Add chicken stock, bring to a boil, reduce heat to low and simmer for 1-2 minutes. Add cabbage, noodles and bell pepper.

Divide among 4 warm soup bowls and garnish with chives.

SERVES: 4   FAT per serving: 3.4 g

Consume the bulk of calories early in the day rather than at night to aid in proper digestion.

TOMATO CLAM SOUP

2	sprays of vegetable oil	2
1	small onion, chopped	1
2	stalks celery, chopped	2
5 cups	prepared chicken stock (powdered)	1.2 L
1 cup	stewed tomatoes	250 ml
1/2 cup	shell pasta	125 ml
1/2 tsp	dried sweet basil	2 ml
1	8 oz / 250 ml can of clams with juice	1
	salt and pepper	

Heat soup kettle with sprays of oil. Sauté vegetables for 3 minutes. Add broth and bring to a boil.

Add tomatoes and pasta and simmer until tender. Season to taste with salt, pepper and basil. Add clams and juice and heat through.

Serve with a wedge of lemon.

SERVES: 6   FAT per serving: 1.7 g

I usually garnish my soups with a dollop of skim milk yogurt or low fat sour cream. Sprinkle with chives, parsley or cilantro for colour and taste.

YUMMY CLAM CHOWDER

2 cups	potatoes, scrubbed and cubed	500 ml
2 cups	cauliflower, cubed	500 ml
1 cup	onion, finely chopped	250 ml
2 1/2 cups	chicken stock	625 ml
1/2 tsp	dill weed	2 ml
1/2 tsp	marjoram	2 ml
1 tsp	chicken stock powder	5 ml
2 tbsp	cornstarch	25 ml
1/3 cup	water	75 ml
1 cup	buttermilk	250 ml
1	10 oz / 298 ml can clams with juice	1
2 tbsp	green onion tops	25 ml

Combine potatoes, cauliflower, onion and chicken stock and cook in soup pot for 15 minutes or until potatoes are tender. Remove from heat and mash, leaving some chunks.

Add dill weed, marjoram and chicken broth powder. Combine cornstarch and water and stir into soup. Heat until thickened. Add buttermilk and clams.

Garnish with green onion tops.

SERVES: 6 - 1 cup each   FAT per serving: 1.5 g

Chapter 7

VEGETABLE SOUPS

ASSORTED WILD MUSHROOM SOUP 86

CARAWAY CABBAGE SOUP 87

"CLEAR OUT THE CRISPER" SOUP 88

EASY ONION SOUP 89

GARLIC AND WATERCRESS SOUP 90

ITALIAN STYLE ONION SOUP 91

MINESTRONE SOUP 92

LEEK AND POTATO SOUP 94

MINESTRONE SOUP WITH KALE 95

OLD FASHIONED CORN CHOWDER 96

ORANGE TOMATO SOUP 97

QUICK CABBAGE SOUP 98

RUSSIAN BORSCHT 99

SIMPLE GARLIC SOUP 100

SUCCOTASH CHOWDER 101

TOFU AND EGG WHITE SOUP 102

WHISKEY CHANTERELLE SOUP 103

ALL SOUP STOCKS USED IN THIS BOOK ARE MADE FROM POWDERED MIXES BECAUSE THEY ARE LOWER IN FAT.

ASSORTED WILD MUSHROOM SOUP

This is a very elegant recipe, perfect for dinner parties.

4 oz	egg noodle pasta	125 g
2	sprays of oil	2
2 tbsp	flour	25 ml
1 1/2 lbs	assorted mushrooms eg. shitake, oyster, chanterelle, white	750 g
4	cloves garlic, minced	4
3 tbsp	sherry	50 ml
2 cups	endive, roughly chopped	500 ml
1/2 cup	cilantro, chopped	125 ml
1/4 tsp	hot sauce	1 ml
5 cups	prepared beef stock (powdered)	1.2 L
	salt and pepper to taste	

Cook pasta according to package directions. Drain and set aside.

In a large saucepan, heat oil sprays over medium heat. Sprinkle flour over mushrooms and add to saucepan. Sauté mushrooms for 3 minutes.

Add garlic and sherry and cook until mushrooms are wilted. Add endive, cilantro, hot sauce, salt and pepper to taste.

Add the stock and simmer for 5 minutes. Add the pasta and serve.

SERVES: 4   FAT *per serving: 1.5 g*

CARAWAY CABBAGE SOUP

5 cups	tomato juice	1.2 L
1 1/2 cup	cabbage, chopped coarsely	375 ml
1/2 cup	onion, chopped fine	125 ml
1/2 cup	celery, sliced	125 ml
1	bay leaf	1
1 tsp	caraway	5 ml
1 tsp	garlic, chopped	5 ml
1 tbsp	red wine vinegar	15 ml
2 tbsp	vegetable stock powder	25 ml
2 tbsp	green onion, tops chopped	25 ml

Bring tomato juice to a simmer. Add cabbage, onion, celery, caraway, bay leaf, garlic and vinegar and simmer for one hour.

Before serving, remove bay leaf and season with the vegetable stock powder.

Sprinkle chopped onions into serving bowls.

SERVES: 4   FAT per serving: 0.5 g

Become a "nibbler", not a "gobbler".

"CLEAR OUT THE CRISPER" SOUP

This recipe is great for a day when there is "nothing in the fridge" except leftovers; you don't feel like grocery shopping but the family is hungry...

2-3	carrots, chopped	2-3
2-3	celery stalks, chopped	2-3
1	onion, chopped	1
1	turnip, optional	1
6 cups	water	1.5 L
1 cup	lentils	250 ml
1	bay leaf	1
1	14 oz / 398 ml can tomatoes	1

In a large soup pot, sprayed with oil, add carrots, celery stalks and the onion. If there are any leftover turnips, add them as well.

Add water, bay leaf, lentils, and tomatoes to the pot and simmer for 45 minutes. Remove the bay leaf. Season to taste with salt and pepper.

You can add any other vegetables you might want to use up - e.g. broccoli or lettuce.

SERVES: 4   FAT per serving: 0.5 g

EASY ONION SOUP

2 tbsp	apple juice	25 ml
1 cup	onion, sliced	250 ml
1 tsp	soy sauce	5 ml
3/4 tsp	onion powder	3 ml
3 cups	prepared beef stock (powdered)	750 ml
3 tbsp	parmesan cheese	50 ml
2 tbsp	fresh chives, minced	25 ml

Combine apple juice and onion in a soup pot and sauté. Add to soup pot, soy sauce, onion powder and beef stock. Simmer for 30 minutes.

Serve in bowls topped with cheese and a sprinkle of chives.

SERVES: 4   FAT per serving: 1.5 g

Fresh food tastes are memorable, satisfying and easy to prepare every day.

GARLIC AND WATERCRESS SOUP

6 cups	water	1.5 L
2	cloves of garlic, peeled and whole	2
1	bay leaf	1
1 1/2 tsp	dried thyme	7 ml
2 tsp	fresh parsley, coarsely chopped	10 ml
3	potatoes, peeled and diced	3
1 tbsp	tarragon vinegar	15 ml
1 tbsp	dijon mustard	15 ml
1 cup	skim evaporated milk	250 ml
2 1/2 cups	watercress, coarsely chopped	625 ml
2	green onions, finely chopped	2

Place water, garlic, bay leaf, thyme, parsley and potatoes in soup pot. Bring to a boil, lower the heat and simmer for 1 hour.

Remove from heat and stir, reserve the broth. Discard the bay leaf. Mash the potato mixture and return it to soup pot and pour in 3/4 cup of broth. Stir over medium heat.

Stir in the vinegar, mustard, milk, watercress and green onion.

Simmer for 30 seconds until watercress has wilted. Adjust seasoning and serve with a dollop of yogurt, if desired.

SERVES: 4   FAT per serving: 0.3 g

ITALIAN STYLE ONION SOUP

3	sprays of vegetable oil	3
4 lbs	yellow onions, thinly sliced	2 kg
2 tsp	sugar	10 ml
1	bottle dry white wine	750 ml
4 cups	prepared vegetable stock (powdered)	1 L
1	cinnamon stick	1
4 cups	very stale Italian or French bread, cubed	1 kg
	fresh chives	
	freshly grated parmesan cheese	
	salt to taste	

Heat a heavy soup pot with the sprays of oil over medium heat. Add the onions and toss. Cover tightly, reduce heat to low and cook onions for 30 minutes or until they are just beginning to colour.

Remove cover and increase the heat to medium and cook until onions are amber - about 45 minutes. Sprinkle with the sugar and a little salt. Stir often until the sugar melts and the onions are caramelized.

Add the wine, broth and cinnamon stick. Bring to a boil, reduce heat and simmer gently for 1 hour. Add bread to soup and continue cooking until bread disintegrates - stir frequently.

Discard the cinnamon stick and serve. Garnish with chives and parmesan cheese.

SERVES: 4   FAT per serving: 3.9 g

MINESTRONE SOUP

This is a very large recipe, so you can freeze half of it and you have some ready-made dinners.

2		sprays of oil	2
1		large onion, sliced thin	1
1 cup		celery, finely chopped	250 ml
1 cup		carrots	250 ml
2 tsp		garlic, chopped	10 ml
1 cup		green cabbage, shredded	250 ml
1 cup		zucchini, diced	250 ml
2 cups		canned tomatoes, crushed	500 ml
4 qts		prepared vegetable stock (powdered)	4 L
1 tsp		dried basil	5 ml
6 oz		small macaroni	150 ml
2		14 oz / 398 ml cans white beans	2
1/4 cup		parsley, chopped	50 ml
		salt and pepper	
		parmesan cheese	

Heat a heavy pot over medium heat that has been sprayed with oil. Add onion, celery, carrots and garlic. Turn down the heat and sweat them until they are tender.

Add cabbage and zucchini and sweat another 3 minutes. Add tomatoes, stock and basil.

Bring to a boil, reduce heat and simmer until vegetables are almost cooked. Add the pasta and simmer until cooked. Add the beans and bring soup back to a boil.

Add parsley, season with salt and pepper. Before serving, stir in the parmesan cheese or sprinkle on top.

SERVES: 24   FAT per serving: 0.3 g

When meat is the main dish, keep the portions small to reduce the amount of fat in the meal.

LEEK AND POTATO SOUP

8	medium leeks	8
1	clove garlic	1
8	medium potatoes, peeled and cubed	8
8 cups	prepared chicken stock (powdered)	2 L
2	bay leaves	2
1 cup	skim evaporated milk	250 ml
	salt and freshly ground pepper	
1/4 cup	fresh parsley, minced	50 ml

Trim all but 2 inches of green part from leeks. Cut lengthwise halfway into white part.

Spread apart and wash under cold running water. Slice by hand, crosswise.

In saucepan combine leeks, garlic, potatoes, chicken stock and bay leaves. Simmer until vegetables are tender, for 30 minutes. Remove bay leaves. Add milk and reheat.

Season with salt and pepper to taste. Sprinkle with parsley.

SERVES: 12   FAT per serving: 1.1 g

Fat - a moment on the lips could be pounds on the hips.

MINESTRONE SOUP WITH KALE

1 cup	tomato paste	250 ml
3 cups	water	750 ml
1/4 cup	chicken stock powder	50 ml
1/2 cup	onion, minced	125 ml
1 1/2 tsp	garlic, minced	7 ml
3/4 tsp	basil	3 ml
1/2 tsp	oregano	2 ml
1 1/2 tsp	chili powder	7 ml
1 1/2 cups	potato, peeled and diced	375 ml
3 cups	mixed fresh vegetables (mushrooms, zucchini, peppers, carrots)	750 ml
1/2 cup	pasta bows	125 ml
1 cup	kidney beans, canned	250 ml
1/4 cup	parmesan cheese	50 ml
2 cups	chopped kale	500 ml

Combine tomato paste, water, stock, onion, garlic, basil, oregano and chili powder in a soup pot. Bring to a simmer.

Add potato, vegetables, pasta and kidney beans and simmer until tender. Add chopped kale and cheese and simmer another 6 minutes.

Serve in bowls.

The kale gives the soup a crunchy texture.

SERVES: 6   FAT per serving: 2.6 g

OLD FASHIONED CORN CHOWDER

1 tbsp	light margarine	15 ml
1	medium onion	1
2 cups	canned or fresh corn	500 ml
4 cups	potatoes, cooked	1 kg
4 cups	skim evaporated milk	1 L
1 1/2 tsp	salt	7 ml
dash of	cayenne pepper	dash
	fresh cilantro	

In soup pot, sauté onion and margarine for 5 minutes. Add corn, potatoes and milk and bring to a boil. Add seasonings and serve.

Garnish with fresh cilantro.

SERVES: 6   FAT per serving: 0.9 g

Raise your fat content consciousness.

ORANGE TOMATO SOUP

Serve in cups as a delicious starter.

3 cups	orange juice	750 ml
3 cups	tomato juice	750 ml
1/2 cup	sherry	125 ml
1/4 cup	lemon juice	50 ml
1 cup	prepared chicken stock (powdered)	250 ml
	dash of sugar	
	dash of cardamom	
	dash of mint	
1 cup	skim evaporated milk	250 ml

Add orange and tomato juice, sherry, lemon juice and chicken stock to saucepan. Bring to a boil. Simmer for 15 minutes.

Remove from heat. just before serving, stir in milk and seasonings and reheat.

Garnish with a sprig of mint.

SERVES: 6-8   FAT per serving: 0.7 g

To prevent any boiling mishaps, just spray the inside of the pot rim slightly with vegetable oil.

QUICK CABBAGE SOUP

This is a quick and inexpensive soup to prepare.

1	onion, large	1
2	sprays of vegetable oil	2
1	small head green cabbage	1
4 cups	prepared vegetable stock (powdered)	1 L
	salt and pepper	

Sauté onion and oil gently in a saucepan until tender.

Grate the cabbage and add it and the stock to the saucepan, bringing to a boil.

Simmer for 15 minutes. Add salt and pepper to taste.

Garnish soup with a dollop of skim milk yogurt and a teaspoon of parsley and caraway seeds, if desired.

SERVES: 6   FAT per serving: trace

Lime or lemon juice will give a "zing" to most vegetable soups.

RUSSIAN BORSCHT

2	sprays of oil	2
1 cup	onions, sliced thin	250 ml
1 cup	leeks, white part, chopped	250 ml
1 cup	cabbage, shredded	250 ml
2 1/2	385 ml cans beets	2 1/2
4 oz	tomato paste	125 ml
4 oz	vinegar	125 ml
2 tbsp	sugar	25 ml
3 1/2 qt	boiling water	3.5 L
	salt and pepper to taste	

Heat soup pot with sprays of oil. Add onion, leeks and cabbage. Cook slowly on low heat for 5 minutes. Drain the beets and save the juice. Chop the beets finely.

Add beets, beet juice, tomato paste, vinegar, sugar and boiling water to onion, leeks and cabbage mixture. Simmer until the vegetables are tender. Season with salt and pepper.

Garnish with low fat sour cream.

Try freezing half this soup for another quick meal.

SERVES: 24   FAT per serving: trace

SIMPLE GARLIC SOUP

For garlic lovers!

1	spray of vegetable oil	1
6-8	cloves garlic, minced	6-8
6 cups	water	1.5 L
4-6 oz	spinach noodles	150 ml
dash	cayenne pepper	dash
1-2	bay leaves	1-2
1 tsp	oregano	5 ml
	parmesan	pinch

In a soup pot, sauté the garlic on medium heat. Add water and bring to a boil. Add bay leaves, oregano, cayenne and finally noodles. Adjust seasoning with salt and pepper.

When noodles are tender, serve. Garnish with a pinch of parmesan cheese and parsley.

SERVES: 4   FAT per serving: trace of fat in cheese

120 g chicken (light meat) with the skin on = 11 grams of fat. Skinless chicken = 2 grams of fat.

SUCCOTASH CHOWDER

2	sprays of oil	2
1	medium onion, finely chopped	1
3	potatoes, peeled, cut into 1/2 inch cubes	3
2 cups	water	500 ml
1 tsp	thyme	5 ml
1/2 tsp	salt	2 ml
1/4 tsp	white pepper	1 ml
3 cups	cooked corn, scooped from the cob or canned corn	750 ml
3-4 cups	skim evaporated milk	750 ml - 1 L
2 cups	cooked baby lima beans or 500 g canned beans	500 ml
1 cup	lean ham, cubed	250 ml
1/4 cup	cilantro	50 ml

In a heavy saucepan, on medium heat, sauté the onion, cooking until soft. Add the potatoes, water, thyme, salt and pepper. Cover and cook for 15 minutes or until potatoes are tender.

Add the corn and milk. Cook uncovered for 10 minutes. Add the lima beans and ham and cook to heat them through.

Sprinkle with cilantro.

SERVES: 6   FAT per serving: 2.9 g

TOFU AND EGG WHITE SOUP

1		spray of vegetable oil	1
1 tsp		soy sauce	5 ml
3/4 cup		onion, finely chopped	175 ml
1 tsp		garlic, minced	5 ml
3/4 cup		celery, diced	175 ml
1 1/2 cups		prepared vegetable stock (powdered)	375 ml
2		egg whites, beaten	2
1/2 lb		tofu, drained	250 g
1/2 cup		green onion, thinly sliced	125 ml

Spray sauce pan and heat it up. Combine soy sauce, onion, garlic and celery in sauce pan and sauté for 2 - 3 minutes.

Add vegetable stock to onion mixture and simmer for 30 minutes. Bring soup to a boil, stir in egg whites and remove from heat. Press liquid out of tofu and slice thinly to look like noodles. Add to soup and reheat.

Garnish with green onions.

SERVES: 12   FAT per serving: 1 g

Instant potatoes make a great thickener for soups.

WHISKEY CHANTERELLE SOUP

Try to use good whiskey in this recipe because it is an elegant soup. Chanterelle mushrooms are a treat, found mostly in gourmet grocery stores.

2 cups	chanterelle mushrooms, sliced	500 ml
3	sprays of oil	3
3 tbsp	flour	50 ml
2 cups	prepared chicken stock (powdered)	500 ml
2 cups	skim evaporated milk	500 ml
1/4 cup	whiskey	50 ml
1 tsp	nutmeg, grated	5 ml
	pinch of thyme	
	salt and pepper to taste	

Sauté sliced mushrooms in oil over medium heat until soft. Add the flour and stir for a few minutes. Slowly add the chicken stock.

Allow to simmer over low heat for 5-10 minutes, stirring frequently. Add the milk and heat thoroughly. Do not boil.

Add the whiskey, nutmeg, salt, pepper and thyme.

SERVES: 4   FAT per serving: 1.5 g

Eating and cooking is all about choices - make the right choices to live healthy.

INDEX

Amazing Medley Bean Soup **8**
Angel-Hair Soup **40,41**
Asparagus Soup **58**
Assorted Wild Mushroom Soup **86**

Black Black-Bean Soup **9**

Caraway Cabbage Soup **87**
Carrot Orange Cream Soup **30**
Chicken Vegetable Soup with Curry **42,43**
Chilled Broccoli Soup **18**
Chilled Garden Soup **19**
Chilled Greek Soup **20**
Chilled Spanish Gazpacho **21**
"Clear Out the Crisper" Soup **88**
Cold Yogurt Soup with Fresh Dill **23**
Cold Cauliflower Soup with Curry **22**
Crab Meat Soup with Savory **74**
Creamy Carrot Soup **31**
Creamy Potato and Broccoli Soup **32**
Creamy Sherry Mushroom Bisque **33**
Creamy Tomato Soup **34**
Creole Peanut Butter Soup **35**
Curried Fish Soup **72,73**

Easy Chilled Avocado Soup **24**
Easy Cream of Corn Soup **36**
Easy Onion Soup **89**

Fennel and White Bean Soup **10,11**
Fish Chowder **75**

Garlic and Watercress Soup 90
Green and White Bean Soup 12

Hallowe'en Pumpkin Soup 59
Henry's Creamy Borscht 60
Hungarian Beef Goulash Soup 44,45

Iced Cucumber Soup 25
Italian Chick-pea Sausage Soup 46,47
Italian Style Onion Soup 91

Japanese Noodle Soup 76

Lamb Soup Stew 48
Leek and Potato Soup 94
Left-over Turkey Soup 49
Lentil Soup 13
Lentil and Brown Rice Soup 14,15

Middle Eastern Chicken Soup 52
Minestrone Soup 92,93
Minestrone Soup with Kale 95
Mulligatawny Soup 50,51

No Fat Quick Blender Soup 61

Old Fashioned Corn Chowder 96
Old Fashioned Split Pea Soup 62
Orange and Grapefruit Soup 26
Orange Tomato Soup 97
Oyster and Clam Chowder 77

Parsnip Soup with Ginger 63
Pear Soup 64

Plain Old Creamy Potato Soup 37
Potato Pick-Me-Up Broth 65

Quick Cabbage Soup 98

Russian Borscht 99
Russian Pink Salmon Soup 78

San Francisco Fish Soup 79
Scallop and Fennel Noodle Soup 80,81
Seven Bean Soup 16
Simple Garlic Soup 100
Spinach Soup 66
Spinach Oyster Purée Soup 67
Succotash Chowder 101
Sweet Red Pepper Soup 68

Tofu and Egg White Soup 102
Tomato Clam Soup 82
Tomato Soup Caribbean Style 69
Turkey Creole Jambalaya 54,55
Turkey Meatball Soup 53

Vichyssoise Soup 27

Whiskey Chanterelle Soup 103

Yellow Squash Soup 70
Yummy Clam Chowder 83

A GIFT IDEA - ORDER FORM

Freedom From Fat Forever
11577 University Avenue
Edmonton, Alberta
T6G 1Z4

*Please send me _____ copies of the
Low-Fat Soups Cookbook.*

*$9.95 per copy plus $1.50 for
Shipping and Handling*

Name:_____

Address: _____

_____

City: _____ Province: _____

Postal Code: _____

Make cheques payable to
"Freedom From Fat Forever"